The Nativity

Written by Bethan Lycett

Illustrated by Hannah Stout

10

Our story of **Christmas** began long ago,

with **Mary** and **Joseph** (but without the snow).

Mary and Joseph were planning a **wedding**,

then they found out where **God's plan** was heading...

An angel told
Mary to not
be afraid,

for she had been
chosen, a plan
had been made.

God would send
a baby inside
of her tummy.

Yes, it was true,
she would
soon be a
mummy!

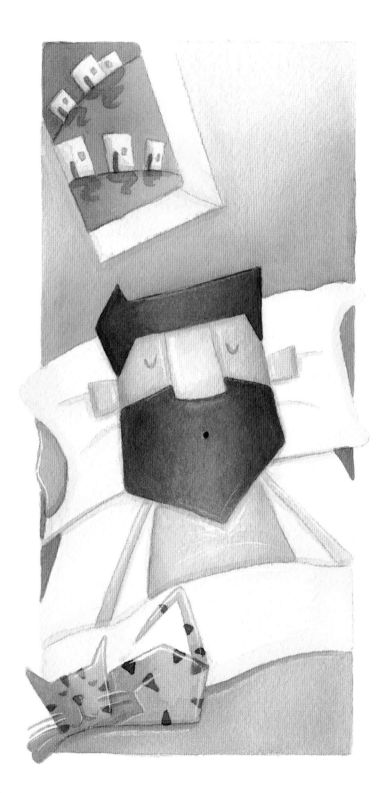

Now Joseph was scared. What would people say?

So an angel brought news in his dream one day.

"What has happened is special, you'll soon be a dad."

And Joseph then trusted it wouldn't be bad.

Mary's cousin
Elizabeth was
really quite old,

too old for a baby is
what she was told.

But God made
it so she could
have a child too,

to prepare the way
for God's Son to
come through.

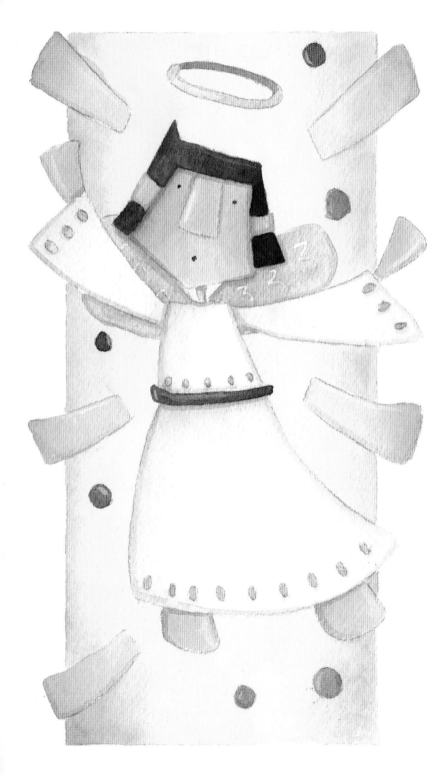

Her husband
was told by an
angel the plan.

He couldn't
believe it, "But I'm
an old man!"

The angel then
told him his voice
would be gone,

as he hadn't believed
what God said
would be done.

For months Zechariah could not make a **sound**,

he had to **write** all he would say on the ground.

At last it was **time** for the baby to come,

and so he wrote down on the ground, "Call him **John**."

A census was
ordered all throughout
the land.

"Let's count
every person," was
Caesar's demand.

So Mary and Joseph
set off for the town,

where the family
of Joseph would be
written down.

The journey to
Bethlehem
was very far,

with no **trains**,
and no **planes**,
no fancy **car**.

They **journeyed**
the 70 miles
they must go,

as **Mary** was
pregnant the trip
was quite **slow**.

But every home
where they hoped
they could stay

was already
taken, "We've no
space today!"

Now the baby
was coming, they
couldn't say no,

the place with the
animals is where
they would go.

Mary's baby was born and laid on a bed,
made out of hay where the animals fed.
"You will call him Jesus," the angel had told her,
"and he will save all of the world when he's older!"

Some **shepherds** nearby were watching their **sheep**, trying their hardest to not fall asleep.

When suddenly an angel appeared in God's **glory** and filled them all in on the **wonderful** story.

Then a big group
of **angels**
appeared to
the crowd,

"**Glory to God**,"
they were praising
out loud.

"The **King**
has been born,
Christ the **Lord**,
here on earth!"

The shepherds
were first to hear
of the **birth**.

"Let's go to see Him," the shepherds declared,

and went down to Bethlehem, just like they'd heard.

Jesus was there like the angel had said,

wrapped in some cloth, in a small manger bed.

After 40 days, to the **temple** they went,

with two **doves** or **pigeons** they had to present.

(A trip to the temple was **needed** by law,

so off to **Jerusalem** they went to explore.)

An old priest called Simeon saw Jesus and knew, that he would bring hope to the world when he grew.

A prophet called Anna came up to them too and gave thanks to God for what Jesus would do.

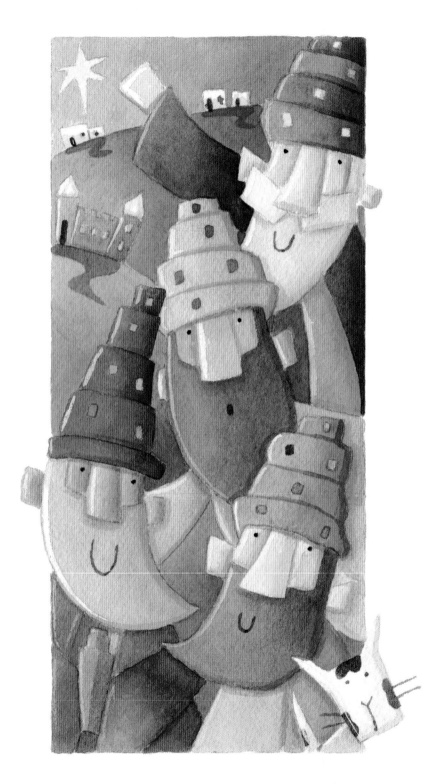

When more time
had passed some
wise men
stopped by.

They had followed
a **star** they had
seen in the **sky**.

They went to the palace
to see the new King,

but King Herod said
he did not know a thing.

"Go find me this child
and I'll worship him too,"

but what Herod told
them just wasn't true.

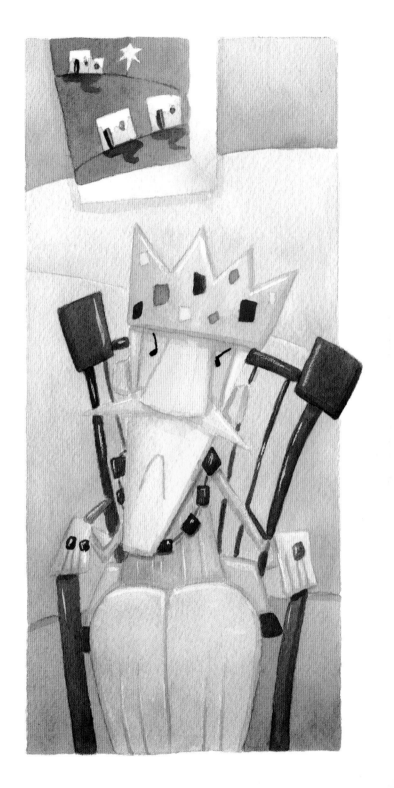

They went on their way and the star rose ahead,
they followed it closely wherever it led.

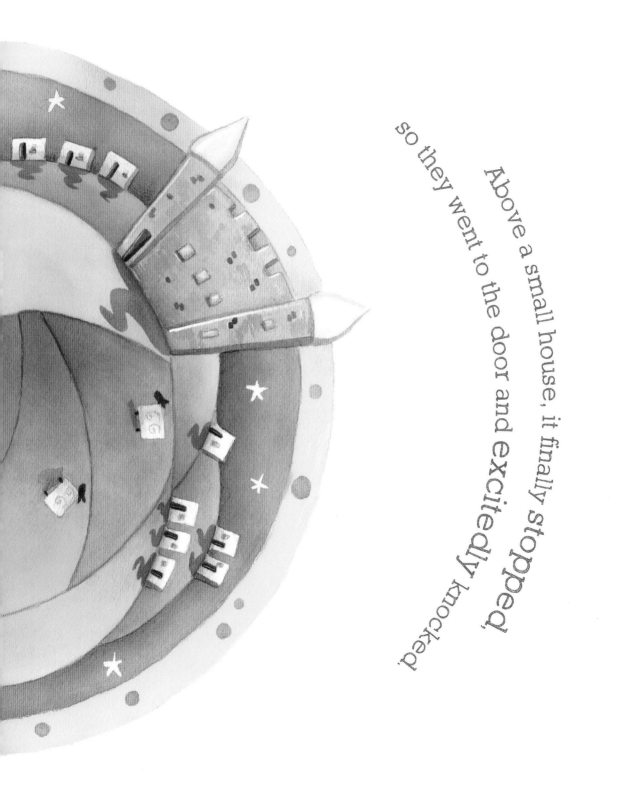

Above a small house, it finally stopped, so they went to the door and excitedly knocked.

We don't know how many **wise men** were there,

but three gifts they brought: gold, frankincense, myrrh.

In a dream, they were told Herod's **terrible** plan,

so a **different** way back to their land they began.

Joseph was warned in a dream the plan too, "Herod will find all the boys under two."

So during the night off to Egypt they fled, and there they would stay until Herod was dead.

When news came to Joseph that all was okay, they journeyed to Nazareth, where they would stay.

The amazing story of Christmas didn't stop after Jesus and his family went to Nazareth. That was just the beginning.

Just as God had planned, Jesus' cousin, John the Baptist, would prepare the people to hear Jesus' message.

From the moment they saw him, Simeon and Anna knew that Jesus would grow up to rescue the whole world and, when he died for us on the cross, that's exactly what he did. The story shows us that God didn't just want rich people, like the wise men, to hear about the birth of Jesus, because the first people to hear were poor shepherds! This is the same today. God wants everyone, rich or poor, to hear about his wonderful Son, Jesus, and to worship him. We may not have gold, frankincense or myrrh to bring to him, but we can give him our hearts and lives today.

If you want to read the story of the
nativity for yourself, you can find
it at the start of both Matthew's
and Luke's gospels in the Bible.

For Leon and Micah

Published by 10Publishing, a division of 10ofThose Limited.

ISBN 978-1-912373-33-8

Typeset by: Diane Warnes

Printed in the China.

10Publishing, a division of 10ofthose.com

Unit C, Tomlinson Road, Leyland, Lancashire, PR25 2DY England

Email: info@10ofthose.com

Website: www.10ofthose.com

More in this series:

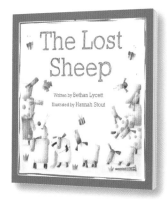

10Publishing is the publishing house of **10ofThose**.
It is committed to producing quality Christian resources that are biblical and accessible.

www.10ofthose.com is our online retail arm selling
thousands of quality books at discounted prices.

For information contact: **sales@10ofthose.com**
or check out our website: **www.10ofthose.com**